FREESTYLIN

Bustin' Out from Law to Life

FREESTYLIN'

Bustin' Out from Law to Life

A creative study of the book of Galatians

by Bryan Belknap

Illustrated by Scott Angle

EMPOWERED
YOUTH PRODUCTS

Standard Publishing
Cincinnati, Ohio

TABLE OF CONTENTS

All Scripture quotations, unless otherwise indicated, are taken from the HOLY BIBLE, NEW INTERNATIONAL VERSION®. NIV®. Copyright © 1973, 1978, 1984 by International Bible Society. Used by permission of Zondervan Publishing House. All rights reserved.

Cover illustration by Scott Angle
Inside design by Dina Sorn
Edited by Dale Reeves and Leslie Durden

© 1999 by Standard Publishing
All rights reserved
Printed in the United States of America

The Standex Publishing Company,
Cincinnati, Ohio.
A Division of Standex International
Corporation.

06   05   04   03   02   01   00   99

5   4   3   2   1

ISBN: 0-7847-0903-3

HOW TO USE THIS BOOK   **7**

LESSON 1   **FREE-FOR-ALL**   **9**
Galatians 1:1-10

LESSON 2   **LOOKIN' ON THE INSIDE**   **17**
Galatians 2:6, 11-21; 3:1-5

LESSON 3   **BRIDGIN' THE GAP**   **25**
Galatians 3:6-14, 21-25

LESSON 4   **UNSHACKLED**   **33**
Galatians 3:26–4:20

LESSON 5   **KICKIN' IT LIVE**   **41**
Galatians 5:1-6, 13-26

LESSON 6   **FREE RIDE**   **49**
Galatians 6:1-10, 14

BONUS SESSION   **ESCAPE FROM ALBADONIA**   **57**
A bonus outreach game that allows students to share Christ's freedom with their friends.

How to Use This Book

Bodies litter the battlefield. Freedom carries a high cost that is paid only in lives lost.

Your students engage in the war for freedom every day. The battle does not rage in a foreign country on a blood-soaked beach. They fight each day in their schools, homes, jobs and even churches. They must fight dearly to hold on to their individuality and the freedom to be themselves. Many fail and trade their freedom for false security, fickle friends and a fake life.

Christians receive the gift of freedom. Not only are we free to be a unique creation, confident in our identity in Christ, but we are also free to live unshackled by sin, the taskmaster which chains the world and refuses to release it from its grasp. Many Christians relinquish their freedom, however, and turn back to sin's bondage. It is your job to ensure that your students do not return to the shackles Jesus unlocked with his death and resurrection.

This problem of legalism was as real in the early church as it is today. Paul writes passionately to the Galatians on the subject, begging them not to forsake Christ's truth for the world's lies. He also warns against putting on "religious" handcuffs. The freedom of Christ extends into the church too. Jesus preached freedom from the Law. We cannot earn our way into Heaven; we can only place our faith in his redemptive sacrifice. Why do we sweat over religious rules and regulations? Doing so sends a mixed message: grace saves us, but you have to follow a bunch of rules to receive that grace.

Paul dispelled this notion in his letter to the Galatians. *Freestylin'* will help you clarify for your students the sufficiency of grace and how faith and the Law work together. They will see the dangers of turning back to a life of sin as well as turning to false doctrine and false gospels. Finally, they will discover how this knowledge affects their everyday life.

Each session in this book is divided into three sections: **Getting Stoked, Dropping In** and **Completing the Run.** Each of these sections contains more than one option or activity for you to use, depending on available resources and the needs of your students. As you prepare to teach, tailor the lesson to fit your group's learning style and focus on the topic your students most need to learn about.

Getting Stoked gets your students connected to the Scripture for the week. Choose whichever option you think would work best with your kids.

Dropping In (In skateboarding lingo, this is when a skater enters the half pipe.) is the meat of the lesson, where the theme is discussed and dissected. Choose

Check This . . .
According to the fair use policy, you can legally use multimedia for educational purposes according to these guidelines: you can use a video clip of 3 minutes or less without securing permission from anyone. If you choose to show more, visit the web site at fairuse.stanford.edu/ for information on whom to contact regarding permission.

Also, two suggested resources, *Shock Wave* videos and *Sanctified Skits*, are available from Ground Zero Productions. You may call them at (310) 390-5611 or visit their web site at www.gbomb.com for more information on their videos, books and worship CD resources.

from these interactive options to involve your students in a meaningful study of God's Word.

Finally, **Completing the Run** gives students something they can go home with and apply immediately. At the conclusion of each study, be sure to distribute copies of the reproducible devotional guide, **Exercising Your Freedom**, to encourage your teenagers to dig into God's Word during the week.

Since the media (especially music and film) make up a large part of students' identities and often shape their culture, we have included at least one **Check This** suggestion with each activity, including music, movie clips or skits that reinforce the point of that particular activity. A warning about these suggestions, especially those involving secular media: preview them first! They are not meant to stand by themselves, but to be woven into your presentation of the material. Without proper explanation before or after, they will become merely entertainment and not a teaching tool. Standard Publishing does not necessarily endorse the entire contents of a particular album or movie.

Galatians speaks directly to the heart of some of the toughest struggles your students face every day, whether they realize they are in the battle or not! This book should effectively equip them for this spiritual warfare in an exciting, engaging way that will stick with them past the close of each week's meeting.

FREE-FOR-ALL 1

Teens receive thousands of messages from hundreds of sources every day. Television, music, chat rooms, teachers, friends, family, church and society are but a few of the places they turn for answers about how to fit in and relate to the world while maintaining their individuality. Whom are they supposed to listen to? How do they discern the good from the bad? Where does Jesus fit in with day-to-day living?

The book of Galatians addresses these issues and more. Paul urges his readers to be clear on the gospel message. Only through rock-solid knowledge of and belief in Christ's redemptive sacrifice will a believer be able to discern truth from fiction. When a teen understands the gospel message, he will "stand for something and not easily fall for anything," as the popular modern proverb states. Anchoring their lives to the Rock is the best thing your students can do during these turbulent years of insecurity, anxiety and awkwardness.

This lesson will explain the heart of the gospel message and put students on the path to discerning whom to listen to among the clamor of voices that calls for their attention.

GETTING STOKED

1 ALIEN ABDUCTION

Before your meeting, draw stars on three of the 3" x 5" index cards, then shuffle them back into the pack. As your students enter, give each one a card, making sure the star cards get handed out. After everyone receives one, instruct the three people with stars on their index cards to come to the front.

Begin by saying, **"These people have been kidnapped by aliens! They will be held prisoner in various spots around the church building. The rest of you are trapped in a force field and must stay in this room until I return with the key. Once you are free, you must search the building to find your friends. You must find them quickly because the aliens have infected their prisoners with a terminal illness, which can be cured only after they are rescued."**

LESSON TEXT
Galatians 1:1-10

LESSON FOCUS
An understanding of the simplicity of the gospel message helps believers discern between truth and falsehood.

LESSON GOALS
As a result of participating in this lesson, students will:
- Gain a clear understanding of the gospel.
- Discover sources of false gospels.
- Identify anything in their lives that is placed before God.
- Discern whom they are pleasing by their lifestyles.

Materials needed:
3" x 5" index cards for each student; Bibles

Check This . . .
Even though it's an old song and video, play Michael W. Smith's "Secret Ambition," from his *i 2 (eye)* album to illustrate Christ's sacrifice for us.

9

Check This . . .
You might play the "Mission Impossible" or "X-Files" theme music during the game to add some suspense.

Hide the students around the church and tell them this terminal illness prevents them from moving or making a sound until someone finds them. Return to your group and let them loose, informing them that their friends cannot move or talk until they are rescued and that anything they move in the building must be returned to its original place.

After the three captives have been rescued, ask everyone to sit for debriefing. Then ask students to respond to these questions:

- **How did it feel to be kidnapped?**
- **How did you feel while searching for your friends?**
- **How did it feel to be saved?**
- **How did you feel when you found them?**

Conclude this activity by saying, **"You just completed a search and rescue mission for some friends who would have died if you hadn't saved them. This is similar to what Jesus did for us on the cross. Humanity was taken captive by sin and infected with the terminal illness of death. Thankfully, Christ performed the ultimate rescue operation by sacrificing himself on the cross in exchange for our sins. Let's read Galatians 1:3-10 to learn how essential this rescue was for our salvation."**

COLLAGE ME BEAUTIFUL

Materials needed:
Magazines; glue sticks; scissors; construction paper; Bibles

Have several magazines, some scissors and glue sticks spread out on a table. Give each student a half piece of construction paper (so it doesn't take as much time to complete). Ask students to make a collage about themselves from the pictures and words they find in the magazines. They have only ten minutes to finish, so they must hurry.

When the ten minutes are up, let students share with the rest of the group what their collage means and why they used the pictures they did. (If your group is too large, break into groups of six to share). When everyone finishes sharing, ask the following questions:

- **Where is God in relationship to the things in your collage?**
- **Why does God hate man putting anything before him?**
- **Are you more devoted to any of the pictures in your collage than you are to God?**
- **Why would anyone value anything more than God?**

Check This . . .
Consider playing one of the following songs which urge us to make God the priority in our lives: "Lay Down Your Gods," from the Kry's album *YOU*; "Gotta Serve Somebody," by Johnny Q. Public on their album *extra ordinary*; or "This World," from Caedmon's Call's self-titled album.

Give each student a small construction-paper cross that you have cut out beforehand. Ask students to glue the crosses in the center of their collages. When they finish, ask them to read Galatians 1:3-10.

Comment, **"Most things in your life are not bad, unless you allow them to come before Christ. The cross should take the center stage of your life, as it does in your collage, and nothing else. How can you put God back on the throne of your life?"**

Allow some time for your students to turn to the person on their left or right. The pairs should discuss ways to follow God wholeheartedly and to dethrone anything in their lives that prevents them from putting God first in their lives.

DROPPING IN

WOULD YOU BELIEVE . . . ?

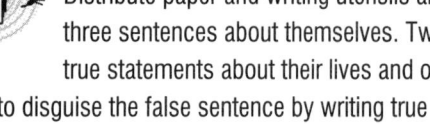

Distribute paper and writing utensils and ask students to write down three sentences about themselves. Two of the sentences should be true statements about their lives and one should be false. They need to try to disguise the false sentence by writing true sentences of things most people would not know about them. Have each student come to the front to read his or her statements, and let the others vote on which statement is the false one. The student should reveal which statement is false before sitting down. (You might want to give a prize for the most shocking true statement.)

Once everyone has taken a turn, ask them to answer the following questions with the person sitting next to them:

- **Has anyone ever lied to you before?**
- **Why would someone try to deceive you like we did in our game?**
- **Has anyone tried to give you a different gospel other than what Jesus preached?**

Hand out copies of the reproducible student sheet found on page 14 of this book. After everyone has had enough time to study the student sheet, encourage them to ask any questions they might have about the religions listed on their sheet. Wrap up the question/answer time by asking:

- **How does a person's view of Jesus tell you whether he or she is teaching a false gospel or not?**
- **What is the difference between Christianity's teaching on how we can get to Heaven and every other religion's path?**
- **Why is Jesus the only way to Heaven?**
- **What are some ways to ensure you do not fall for a different gospel?**
- **How can you witness to someone from another religion?**

Challenge your students to know what they believe, why they believe it and what God says. They live in a multicultural world with multicultural beliefs and they must be knowledgeable, or they may give up their freedom for a cheap imitation.

THE TRUTH IS OUT THERE

To begin this activity, ask everyone to form pairs and spread out around the room.

Say, **"You and your partner are FBI agents. You are on assignment to investigate a bizarre case. The body of a deceased man has disappeared. There are several theories floating around, so we need you to go in and discover the truth. Derive your conclusions from the following reports."**

Ask students to read and discuss clues in the following Scriptures: Mark 15:42-47; Luke 24; Matthew 27:57-66; 28:11-20; and John 20:10–21:25. While they work in pairs, list on the blackboard or a piece of butcher paper these theories, allowing space between them for you to write additional comments:

- *The body was placed in a different tomb.*
- *The man was not really dead, only unconscious.*
- *The body was stolen.*
- *The body came back to life.*

Materials needed:
Writing utensils; slips of paper; reproducible student sheet on page 14 of this book

Check This . . .
Some resources on cults worth checking out are *The Kingdom of the Cults*, by Walter Martin (© 1985, Bethany House Publishers); *Another Gospel*, by Ruth A. Tucker (© 1989, Academie Books); and *What's With the Dudes at the Door? Stuff to Know When the Cults Come Knocking*, by Kevin Johnson and James White (© 1998, Bethany House Publishers).

Check This . . .
Show a clip from *Liar, Liar* (PG-13) which begins at 9 minutes and 30 seconds into the video. A lawyer refuses to lie, and then you will hear several quick lies given by Jim Carrey. Use this clip to demonstrate how people lie and try to deceive others every day.

Check This . . .
Several songs that deal with Jesus' superiority are "Thing Called Jesus," by Big Tent Revival, recorded on their *Open All Nite* album; and "Liquid," which is recorded on Jars of Clay's self-titled album.

Materials needed:
Bibles; chalkboard or butcher paper; chalk or markers

11

Check This . . .
The *Actual Reality* CD-ROM has some hilarious short films using stop-action video and action figures to reenact the possibilities of the disappearance of Jesus' body.

Once everyone has had ample time to discuss and form conclusions, come back together. Walk through the different theories you have written and allow your "agents" to report on why they do or do not support them. After a consensus is reached, ask:

- **If you had been alive when Jesus died on the cross, would you have believed he rose again? Why or why not?**
- **What makes you certain of your faith in Christ?**
- **What are some ways you can increase your faith in Jesus and the truth of his resurrection?**

Conclude by saying, **"As you have concluded, there is overwhelming evidence that Jesus did rise from the dead. This is a fact that you can all stand firm on and use as an anchor point. Also, you are to be commended. Jesus said, '"Blessed are those who have not seen and yet have believed"' (John 20:29). God will definitely reward your belief with an eternity spent with him in Heaven."**

COMPLETING THE RUN

FIREPROOF?

Materials needed:
Magazines or blank paper and markers; matches; metal trash can; fire extinguisher; CD player

Provide either several magazines or several blank sheets of paper and markers. Ask your students to identify the thing or things in their lives that they are putting before God—the things they have traded the true gospel for. If they do not have something that has taken God's place on the throne of their hearts, then encourage them to identify something that could become a problem if they are not careful. Have them find a picture of it in a magazine and tear it out, or draw it with the markers. When everyone finishes, ask a student to read 1 Corinthians 3:13-15 aloud.

Ask:

- **Why do we trade the promise of the eternal gospel for something that will perish?**
- **Will your idol withstand the fire of Judgment Day?**

Take everyone outside into the parking lot. Set a metal trash can out for all to see (in a safe spot you have prepared beforehand). Be sure to have matches or a lighter with you, as well as a fire extinguisher (just in case).

After you have all the students' attention, say something like this: **"We're going to see if what you've chosen to place before God will stand up to the flames."**

Check This . . .
Play one of the following songs while setting fire to the pictures: Squirrel Nut Zippers' song "Hell," from the secular album *Hot!*; "Gasoline," by Skillet, on their self-titled release; or Newsboys' song "Breakfast," recorded on their *Take Me to Your Leader* album.

Have each student come forward and put his or her "idol" to the test by placing the picture in the fire. In order to set the example, you might start by lighting your drawing on fire first. As students come forward one by one and their papers catch fire (make sure they do), they should drop them in the trash can. After every student's idol is ash, say:

"Search your heart this week. Make sure you are not placing anything before God, because this is what will happen to it on Judgment Day—it will burn away. Do not pour your life into something that will simply disappear in an instant. Build upon foundations that will last for eternity."

ENIGMATIC ELUCIDATION

Ask everyone to find a partner, face each other, and follow these specific instructions: **"Extend your right appendage vertically from your torso so it forms a right angle at the joint, with the lower half of the appendage parallel to the earth's crust. Keep your digits closed while extending the opposable digit vertically. Place your epidermis flat against your partner's epidermis, locking opposable digits. Contract the protein strands in your appendage to create a smooth motion toward the stratosphere. Release the muscle tension in your right appendage to return to your previous position. Repeat contracting and releasing as desired."** Hopefully, your students will be shaking hands after following these ridiculously cryptic directions!

Comment, **"Obviously, this is an absurd way to ask someone to shake hands. Sometimes, though, we make simple things in life very difficult. The gift of salvation is one example. It is a free gift, but many people make it incredibly hard to understand."**

Let the partners discuss a time when someone has made something that is simple very difficult. Then ask them to discuss these questions:

- **Why do people make salvation hard to understand?**
- **Why do people try to add rules to a gift that God gives free of charge?**
- **Why doesn't everyone accept God's free gift if it is so accessible?**

Distribute copies of the reproducible student sheet found on page 15 and have students fill it out in order to learn more about the simplicity of the gospel message. When they finish, give the answers to the "technical" explanations. They are as follows: *1. a cup; 2. ice cream; 3. a Frisbee; 4. a bed.*

Have students form groups of three to answer the following:

- **Did you know the gospel was so simple?**
- **What else do you think God requires of you?**
- **Did you know these promises were written specifically for you?**
- **Are there any adjustments you need to make based on these verses?**

Distribute copies of the reproducible student sheet titled "Exercising Your Freedom" that's found on page 16 of this book. You will need to provide seven copies of this sheet for each student, so that they can evaluate each day of the week.

Materials needed:
Reproducible student sheets on page 15, 16 of this book; writing utensils

Check This . . .
Play Lenny Kravitz's "God Is Love" song, from the secular album *Circus*.

Check This . . .
As an example of someone making something more difficult than it needs to be, show a clip from the video, *Better Off Dead*. There is a scene that begins 23 minutes from the opening credits that depicts a math teacher talking in incredibly difficult terminology.

13

WHAT WE BELIEVE

"Jesus answered, 'I am the way and the truth and the life. No one comes to the Father except through me.'"—John 14:6

Many people do not believe this statement by Jesus. Below are some brief descriptions of different religions, each of which takes a different path to God.

	Prophet	Scripture	Who Is God?	Who Is Jesus?	How Do You Get to Heaven?
CHRISTIANITY	several	the Bible	Yahweh	Son of God	by accepting the free gift of salvation that comes from Jesus' sacrificial death
ISLAM	Mohammed	the Koran	Allah	prophet who was sinless, but not God	by living the Five Pillars of the Faith
BUDDHISM	the Buddha	none	yourself	failed Buddhist who suffered	by following the Eightfold Path and achieving Nirvana or Enlightenment
MORMONISM	Brigham Young	the Book of Mormon	several	created by Elohim (a man who attained spiritual enlightenment); died for us	everyone goes, but our works determine which level of Heaven we get into
NEW AGE MOVEMENT	several	various (many "self-help" books are New Age)	all is God/one	master of New Age practices/ the occult	by realizing "we are all God," you become one with the universe and release your spirit
SCIENTOLOGY	L. Ron Hubbard	Dianetics	yourself	a "clear," exemplified in post-resurrection appearances	by becoming "clear" of all negative impressions on your psyche, you are freed from your body to roam the universe
HINDUISM	several	the Vedas (sayings) and the Upanishads (stories)	we are all part of god	not mentioned	by attaining a level of spiritual consciousness, you are released into spiritual bliss
JEHOVAH'S WITNESSES	Charles Russell	New World Translation of the Bible	Jehovah	a perfect man, but not God, who died on a torture stake; Michael the Archangel appeared as the risen Jesus	by emphasis on works because only 144,000 enter Heaven

14 **Lesson 1** ©1999 by The Standard Publishing Company. Permission is granted to reproduce this page for ministry purposes only—not for resale.

SIMPLY SILLY DESCRIPTIONS

Below are a few descriptions of common objects. See if you can figure out what they are by deciphering their "technical" explanation.

1. receptacle for liquefied matter

2. glacially congealed lactose confection

3. synthetic gliding plate of equidistant circumference

4. nocturnal berth for extensive horizontal prostrations

Thankfully, the gospel isn't a secret code that must be deciphered. In fact, it's personalized just for you! Place your name in the blanks below to discover the simple gift God prepared just for you.

"For it is by grace _____ [has] been saved, through faith—and this not from [himself], it is the gift of God—not by works, so that _____ can [not] boast."—Ephesians 2:8, 9

"If _____ confess[es] with _____ mouth, 'Jesus is Lord,' and believe[s] in [his/her] heart that God raised him from the dead, _____ will be saved." —Romans 10:9

"Then he called the crowd to him along with his disciples and said: 'If _____ would come after me, [he] must deny [him]self, and take up [his] cross and follow me." —Mark 8:34

Hopefully, these verses make the gospel clear. If not, be sure to talk to your youth leader immediately after the meeting.

©1999 by The Standard Publishing Company. Permission is granted to reproduce this page for ministry purposes only—not for resale.

Exercising Your Freedom

"Am I now trying to win the approval of men, or of God? Or am I trying to please men? If I were still trying to please men, I would not be a servant of Christ."—Galatians 1:10

How does this verse fit your life? Fill your weekly schedule into the chart below. Beside each hourly time slot in your day, indicate whether what you're doing then is glorifying God or not. Be honest! Glorifying God with your life does not mean spending every hour in church, but you should fill your life with things that bring honor to God. This can be playing basketball, hanging out at church, studying, working or playing drums. It all depends on whether God receives the glory for your activity. If some time slots do not bring glory to God, pray about it, asking the Holy Spirit to reveal whether you need to quit that activity or how you can shift the focus back to God.

DAY	ACTIVITY	DOES THIS GLORIFY GOD?
7:00 A.M.		
8:00 A.M.		
9:00 A.M.		
10:00 A.M.		
11:00 A.M.		
Noon		
1:00 P.M.		
2:00 P.M.		
3:00 P.M.		
4:00 P.M.		
5:00 P.M.		
6:00 P.M.		
7:00 P.M.		
8:00 P.M.		
9:00 P.M.		
10:00 P.M.		
11:00 P.M.		

LOOKIN' ON THE INSIDE

Teens are warned about all the pitfalls they will face while en route to adulthood: greed, peer pressure, drug and alcohol abuse, failure, sexual immorality. Few people, however, warn them of the spiritual pitfalls they must avoid on their way to becoming a man or woman of God. Many times, they mistakenly assume following Jesus is a cakewalk when compared to the minefield of "real life."

Though following Christ gives hope and peace to endure daily trials, it often makes daily living more complicated. Christians face "spiritual" temptations that non-Christians never consider. Being set apart with Christ makes believers special, but it also opens the door for pride and self-righteousness to enter into their lives. Teens must not only be clear on the gospel, but also understand perfectly where they fit into that gospel and how their new life affects their relationships with others. It is easy to be misled by well-intentioned believers into battles God does not care about.

This study should begin to establish the freedom your students have in Christ—freedom both from being judgmental and self-righteous and from being tossed back and forth by the changing whims of the world.

GETTING STOKED

STANDING FIRM

Get a paint can or reinforced plastic bucket that can support a person's weight but does not provide much standing space. Place the bucket upside down in the middle of a large, clear space in your room. Ask a volunteer to stand on the bucket and the rest of your students to gather in a tight group on one side of the bucket. Say: **"Our volunteer is going to try to stand strong against the crowd. I want everyone to walk past the bucket in a large group. You cannot shove him off the bucket or run right over him. Simply walk past him like you are on a busy city street or walking through the packed-out halls of your school between classes."**

Try the experiment to see if the bucket person maintains his balance and stands firm against the flow of the crowd. Give each student an opportunity to stand on the bucket. (If your group is large, break it up into two or three groups with buckets so every student has a chance to stand. Have students who own a dog gather

LESSON TEXT
Galatians 2:6, 11-21; 3:1-5

LESSON FOCUS
Learning how to identify with Christ rather than with the world is essential to true freedom in Jesus.

LESSON GOALS
As a result of participating in this lesson, students will:
- Stand firm in their convictions.
- Not get caught up in "religion."
- Not judge others by appearance.
- Discover what it means to die to self.

Materials needed:
Paint can; Bibles

Check This . . .
A couple of secular songs that deal with this topic are "I Won't Back Down," by Tom Petty and the Heartbreakers, recorded on their *Greatest Hits* album and REM's song "Stand," from their album *Green*.

17

Check This . . .
Perform the skit "Go With the Flow," from *Sanctified Skits, Vol. II.* (Available from Ground Zero Productions at (310) 390-5611 or on their web site at www.gbomb.com.) This skit portrays a game show where one of your students is tempted to go along with a bunch of celebrities in doing things that are wrong.

Materials needed:
Bibles

in one group, those who have a cat in another and those with no pets in a third group.) Once everyone has had a turn, ask them to break into groups of four, perhaps by the color of their eyes (each group has four different individuals with blue, brown, green and hazel eyes). Allow groups some time to discuss these questions:

- **How did it feel standing on the bucket?**
- **Was it difficult to stand firm with everyone going the opposite way?**
- **Do you ever feel like your life is like this?**

Conclude this activity by saying, **"The early church had several people saying different things about what being a Christian means. Paul challenged the Galatians to stand strong in their faith and not be swayed by everyone who comes along saying something different. Read what Paul said in Galatians 2:1-6, 11-21 and 3:1-5 out loud in your groups."**

Ask students to respond to this question:

- **What did Paul stand strong against?**

WHAT IF?

Play "What If?" with your youth group by breaking your students into groups of three to five. First, ask the question, **"If you could be anything you wanted, who would you be?"** Give students three to five options, which are as follows: a TV star from a popular TV show (you choose); a world-class model; a rock star; a famous athlete; or a doctor who discovers the cure for AIDS. Have them gather in groups based on their responses to the question.

Once they are in their separate groups, ask, **"What would the world be like today if the Germans had won World War II? How would things be different in the United States?"** Let the groups discuss this change in history for about five minutes. Allow a few group representatives to come forward and present their report on what the world would be like if it were run by Hitler.

Once they finish reporting, ask them to resume their groups and discuss this question: **"What would the world be like today if Jesus had not died on the cross and risen again? How would we get to Heaven?"** Give groups approximately ten minutes to compile their reports this time. Ask a different representative from each group to come forward and share their findings with everyone.

Close this activity by saying, **"Thankfully, Christ *did* go to the cross. Paul says in Galatians that without Christ's death and resurrection, we would be subject to the law. Christ's death is what sets us free. Read what he said in Galatians 2:1-6, 11-21 and 3:1-5 right now."**

Check This . . .
Play Johnny Q Public's song "As I Pray," from their *ExtraOrdinary* album. This song details Christ's struggle in Gethsemane with going to the cross.

DROPPING IN

YOU SAY TOMATO

Have the entire group stand up and cluster in the center of the room. Then say, **"I am going to list several choices for you. I want you to answer the following questions by moving to the side of the room that fits your preference."**

Begin to give several different preferences your students might have and direct them to one side of the room or the other, depending on their choice. Some examples of preferences are: diet soft drinks vs. regular soft drinks; bagels vs. toast;

Materials needed:
Bibles; marker board and marker

18 Lesson 2

romantic movies vs. action movies; pepperoni pizza vs. vegetarian pizza; rock music vs. rap music, etc. Your students should be moving from one side of the room to the other, according to their preferences. Once you present five to ten examples, have everyone sit down in their seats.

Comment, **"We have just made some choices about preferences we have. No one is right or wrong; we're just unique. There are also some preferences in the way people conduct their church: music style, how we dress, the time of day we worship, etc. None of these things affect our salvation or relationship with Christ; they just indicate how we feel comfortable worshiping God. Let's take a look at a preference that some people believed was a command during Paul's time."**

Ask your students to turn to their neighbor and to read Genesis 17:9-14 followed by Romans 2:25-29. Ask them to answer the following questions:

- **What was circumcision a symbol of?**
- **What was more important than physical circumcision?**
- **Why do you think the Jews and the Gentiles had such a debate over this issue?** (Refer to Galatians 2:3-6, 15, 16; 3:2-5 for help.)
- **Are there any issues in our church that cause dissension like circumcision did for the early Christians?** Allow students to make comments, writing them down on the marker board. Discuss whether or not each issue is a preference or a nonnegotiable of faith.
- **How should we decide which things are preferences and which ones are commands?**
- **How can we find harmony in our differences?**
- **Does God like diversity in worship?**

THE LIVING DEAD

Ask your students to form groups of four and to briefly tell each other about a time in their lives when they had to lay down their wants and desires and do what someone else wanted. Once they finish, have a volunteer in each group reread Galatians 2:17-21 out loud. Then have groups discuss these questions:

- **Is it difficult to put aside our own desires in favor of someone else's?**
- **Paul says we need to "die to self." What does he mean by that?**
- **How were we crucified with Christ?**
- **Why do we still sin if our sins were crucified?**

When groups have finished, share the following: **"A well-known Christian author and speaker (Gary Smalley) has asked the question, 'Would you rather have a 110-voltage electrical current running through your body or a 220-voltage current?' He is referring to the 'electrical' power of God. The 110-voltage current is Galatians 1:10, which deals with trying to please men; but the 220-voltage power is found in our study today, in Galatians 2:20, where Paul speaks of the power of Christ living within us because we have died to ourselves."** Ask students, **"Which kind of power would you rather have in the Christian life?"**

Distribute copies of the reproducible student sheet located on page 22 and ask students to fill it out. Give them approximately five minutes to do so. When everyone is done, hand each person a shoe box or something else that can be sealed

Check This . . .
Play one of the following songs to underscore the lesson: Rich Mullins' song "Creed," from his *Liturgy, Legacy and a Ragamuffin Band* album; or Carolyn Arends' song "Feel Free," from her album *Feel Free*.

Materials needed:
Bibles; writing utensils; shoe boxes (or something else they can seal a piece of paper inside); reproducible student sheet on page 22 of this book

Check This . . .
A great song to play while students are working on the student sheets and placing them in the "coffins" is "Some Kind of Zombie," recorded by Audio Adrenaline on their album by the same name.

Check This . . .
Show the clip in *Star Trek II: The Wrath of Khan* that begins at one hour and 37 minutes from the opening credits. The scene shows Spock "dying to self" so others can live.

Materials needed:
Bibles; several costumes

Check This . . .
Play Randy Stonehill's song "Rachel Delavoryas," from his album *Stories* or the song "Bus Driver," from the self-titled debut album by Caedmon's Call.

Check This . . .
Show "The Mansion," from *Shock Wave, Vol. 4* (a young man shows his hypocrisy by gloating about the beautiful exterior of his home, and we later find the interior completely trashed); or "Roomies," from *Shock Wave, Vol. 4* (this fake trailer for a documentary exposes many of the stereotypes people have about Christians).

and become a "coffin" for their reproducible. (Other possibilities include large match boxes, milk cartons and soft drink cans.) Ask students to take their completed sheets, stick them inside the "coffins" you have provided and seal them. Make a graveyard at the front of the room with the coffins and ask students to return to their groups.

Comment, **"You have now killed your 'selves.' You have laid down your lives and now stand empty, ready for Christ to fill you up. Do you think this means God will take away the things you enjoy doing?"**

Ask groups to consider these questions:
- **Does God want to take away all our fun?**
- **How do you have fun and still remain dead to the world?**
- **How does this affect the way we need to live?**

Allow the groups time to discuss how "dying to self" changes their lives today, what changes they need to make in their lives and how they can help each other stick to their commitments. Encourage them to pray for wisdom and strength in their daily quest to die to themselves.

Close this activity by saying, **"Christ promised an abundant life here on earth when we follow him (John 10:10). By laying down our lives now, we can receive the best that God has prepared for us."**

COMPLETING THE RUN

HOW TYPICAL!

Have one of your adult leaders model four or five different stereotypical costumes (cowboy, skateboarder, homeless person, cheerleader, jock, surfer, etc.) for your students. Ask students to identify each stereotype and then describe how that person would typically talk, where they would live, what kind of job they would have and any other characteristic they associate with that costume.

Once the "fashion show" is over, have your leader come out in his or her regular clothes and stand in front of the group. Ask students to describe the leader's personality, likes, dislikes and any other information about his or her character.

Say, **"Every person you saw tonight was** (leader's name). **The only difference was the clothing he (she) wore. Each time, though, you saw a completely different person and assumed a great many things about him (her) simply by the way he (she) was dressed. We tend to judge people on their exteriors and by what they wear without really getting to know them."**

Break everyone into groups of four or five, perhaps by some clothing and appearance distinctions, such as sweatshirts, T-shirts and buttoned shirts; or short hair, really short hair and long hair. Have them read Galatians 2:6 out loud in their groups. Then say, **"Share with your group a time you judged someone and later found out you were wrong in your assumptions."** After they have shared their stories, ask, **"How did you feel when you realized you were mistaken about that person?"**

"Now, share with your group about a time when someone judged you incorrectly—thought you were different than you were." Allow time for them to tell their stories, then have them discuss these questions:
- **Why did that person assume you were that way?**

20   Lesson 2

• **Were you able to change their opinion? If so, how?**

Close this activity by saying, **"To judge on appearance may be natural, but it is not right. Pray with your group for an open heart and mind when meeting people and the opportunity to build friendships and not just form opinions."**

DON'T JUDGE A BOOK

Hand out copies of the reproducible student sheet located on page 23 of this book and ask your students to fill it out and hand it in when finished. Quickly look them over and ask the "most righteous" people to come forward. Let them sit in the front, and give each of them a candy bar or some other desirable gift.

Comment, **"These people deserve special treatment because they are the best examples of what a Christian is. From now on, they will sit in the front row at our meetings."**

Before a riot starts, ask everyone to reread Galatians 2:11-13. Then discuss these questions with the entire group:

• **Why did Paul oppose Peter?**
• **How were the Jews being hypocrites?**
• **Do we ever judge other Christians this way? How?**
• **Why is this wrong?**
• **Do we ever do that in our youth group?**

Talk about the need to root out any hypocrisy infesting the youth group and brainstorm with your group ways to keep such a situation from happening again. Have a time of prayer where everyone thanks God for accepting a bunch of sinners as righteous and requests help in remembering that everyone is a sinner when standing before God.

Distribute copies of the reproducible student sheet titled "Exercising Your Freedom" that's found on page 24 of this book. Encourage your students to honestly deal with this week's challenge.

Materials needed:
Bibles; reproducible student sheets on pages 23, 24 of this book; writing utensils; candy

21

What I Like

Please fill in your favorite for each item below:

Food _____   Dessert _____

Movie _____   Singer/Band _____

TV Show _____   Sport _____

Friend _____   Vacation Spot _____

Beverage _____   Hobby _____

Holiday _____   School Subject _____

Career _____   Brand of Clothes _____

Season _____   Video Game _____

Magazine _____   Shoe Brand _____

22   Lesson 2   ©1999 by The Standard Publishing Company. Permission is granted to reproduce this page for ministry purposes only—not for resale.

"MoSt RighTeoUS" Report

Please answer the following questions truthfully and turn this sheet in when you finish.

Name: _____

- How many years have you been a Christian?

- How many years have you attended this church?

- How often do you read the Bible?

- How many Sundays in a row have you been to church?

- Have you ever missed church on Easter Sunday?

- Did you pray today?

- Have you ever told anyone about Jesus?

Exercising Your Freedom

"Be perfect, therefore, as your heavenly Father is perfect."—Matthew 5:48

This week, you are going to try to live perfectly according to God's law. Pray that the Holy Spirit would point out to you any time during the day that you break God's law. Keep this page in your notebook at school and write down any times that you fail. Keep the list every day this week. Before you go to bed each night, review it and answer the questions.

• Were you perfect today?

Monday

Tuesday

Wednesday

Thursday

Friday

Saturday

• Do you think you can live a perfect life every single day of your life?

• Why do you not have to worry about living a perfect life?

Thank God tonight for setting you free from the burden of the law and giving you a path to Heaven other than your own good works.

24   Lesson 2   ©1999 by The Standard Publishing Company. Permission is granted to reproduce this page for ministry purposes only—not for resale.

BRIDGIN' THE GAP

"How do I reconcile faith and law?" This question had the apostle's head spinning, and certainly confuses your students. They constantly struggle with keeping the "rules" of the church while claiming the redeeming, forgiving grace of the gospel. Where is the line between keeping the rules and being comfortable with the fact that this is impossible?

Paul understood this tension and built a bridge between faith and the Law in chapter three of Galatians. God accepts us because of our faith in his Son, nothing more. Some teens take this fact as their license to sin and merely ask for forgiveness later. Paul is very clear (as you should be) that this is not proper. If they love Jesus, they will obey what he says! It's a fine line to walk—trying to obey God's commands, but realizing this is impossible, so instead relying on our faith in Christ for salvation.

This session should teach your students the difference between the Law and faith and how these two institutions actually work together to create a framework for Christian life.

GETTING STOKED

1 JUDGE JEHOVAH

Hand out 3" x 5" index cards to each student. Have one sin written on each card. These sins should vary from those with grave consequences like murder, blasphemy and rape to those that we categorize as "no big deal" like lies, gossip and envy. Have each person come to the front and be the defendant on trial for the sin on the card. After reading the 3" x 5" card out loud, the group must then vote on whether that person should go to jail or not. Separate the group into two sides of the room: those sentenced to jail on one side and the ones free to walk the streets on the other side.

After everyone has been separated, ask them to come before the judge again. This time, God is judging their sins and whether or not they will be allowed into Heaven because of them. This time, everyone should be standing together in the group headed for Hell. Comment, "**It takes only one sin to condemn us to eternal separation from God.**" Ask students to grapple with these questions:

- **What makes God's "courtroom" different from a United States courtroom?**

LESSON TEXT
Galatians 3:6-14, 21-25

LESSON FOCUS
Understanding the difference between living by faith and living by the Law is critical for the spiritual growth of a believer.

LESSON GOALS
As a result of participating in this lesson, students will:
- Understand the differences between the Law and faith.
- Discover God's promise to Abraham.
- Realize how Christ created a bridge between faith and the Law.

Materials needed:
Bibles; 3" x 5" index cards

Check This . . .
Show the video segment "Sin Scale," from *Shock Wave, Vol 1*. This clip shows a movie theater where the scale that people normally rank sins with has been flipped upside down.

Check This . . .
Play Black Eyed Sceva's song "Handshake," from their album *Way Before the Flood.*

Materials needed:
Bibles; desk; mat (optional)

Check This . . .
Play Big Tent Revival's song "Faith of a Little Seed," from their self-titled album or Sixpence None the Richer's song "Trust," from their album *The Fatherless and the Widow*.

Check This . . .
Show the video clip "Rappelling," from *Shock Wave, Vol. 2*. In this segment, people anchor their ropes to (put their faith in) different things.

Materials needed:
Bibles

- **How is God's view of sin different from ours?**
- **Is it possible to keep all of God's law?**
- **Is it fair that one sin excludes us from Heaven?**

Conclude this activity by saying, **"Sin separates us from God. There is not one person who deserves eternal life on his own merit. Please read Galatians 3:6-14, 21-25 along with me."**

DO YA TRUST ME?

Find a desk or something else sturdy enough to support the weight of someone standing on it. Have eight of your students stand on the ground in front of the table while another student stands on the table with his back to them. The eight students should face each other and, forming two lines of four, hold their arms out straight in front of them, palms up, alternating their arms with the person across from them. Thus, there should be sixteen arms held out so a flat "bed" is formed beneath the person on the table. (The bed of arms should be level and have small gaps.)

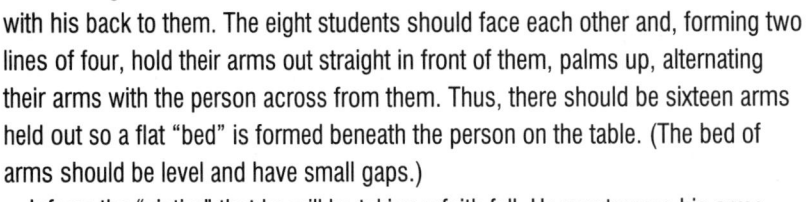

Inform the "victim" that he will be taking a faith fall. He must cross his arms across his chest and fall back flat into the arms of the students below. He MUST NOT bend in the middle (sticking out his rear end), or he will fall through the "bed" of arms. (You might have a mat or something else soft that will soften a "drop," or possibly do this outside on the grass.) After falling safely into the arms of his friends, the volunteer will take someone's place in the "bed," giving the person he replaced a chance to experience the faith fall. Continue "falling" until everyone has a chance to participate. (If your group is large, break into several faith fall groups. Be sure to have an adult in each group for safety reasons.) After everyone takes a turn, bring the group back together and discuss these questions:

- **Was it hard to trust others to catch you?**
- **How did it feel to fall backwards?**
- **Is it easy to trust that God will catch you and protect you?**
- **Has God ever asked you to take a "faith fall" of any kind during your life?**

Comment, **"The apostle Paul talks about Abraham, faith and its place in our lives. Please read Galatians 3:6-14, 21-25 now."**

DROPPING IN

MIND THROUGH MATTER

Ask everyone to get a partner and spread out around the room. The older student in each pair should lie down flat on the floor on his or her stomach with arms stretched out in front. Instruct the partners to stand in front of their prostrate friends and lift their arms up off the floor as high as they can without hurting them. They must hold their arms aloft for twenty to thirty seconds. When the time is up, they should SLOWLY lower their friends' arms back down flat on the floor, which should create the sensation that their arms are passing right through the floor. Have the partners trade places and repeat the process. (You may need to do it a third time for the people who didn't originally feel the sensation.) When everyone finishes, ask students to resume their seats.

Comment, **"Even though your senses told you your arms went through the floor, you knew they did not. (If not, I have some beach-front property I'd like**

26   Lesson 3

to sell you!) Your faith in the floor being solid overpowered what your brain told you. Faith sometimes involves believing something, even when your brain tells you something different."

Have everyone break into small groups of three or four students. Ask them to read Genesis 12:1-5 and talk about these questions:

- **What was so crazy about Abraham moving?**
- **Abraham was justified before God preceding Christ's death on the cross. How was that possible?**
- **Would you have done what Abraham did?**

Next, ask students to read Genesis 22:1-19 and discuss:

- **Why would Abraham kill his only son?**
- **Why did God test Abraham's faith?**
- **What would have happened if Abraham had not followed God's instructions?**
- **Why is following God so difficult sometimes?**
- **Do people always understand and support acting on faith?**

Point out Genesis 23:1, 2 to them, stressing that Sarah was so upset with Abraham that she did not live with him for the rest of her life. Abraham stepped out in faith, and this time he stepped out alone since his wife would not join him.

Ask, **"Why is Abraham commended throughout the Bible and history for his faith? Can you become faithful like Abraham?"**

A TEST OF GRACE

Distribute copies of the reproducible student sheet located on page 30 of this book and allow ten minutes for students to complete it. When time is up, have everyone trade papers to grade it.

The answers are as follows:

1) Amon	*6) Leigh Brackett & Lawrence Kasdan*
2) Gifford Pinchot	*7) Grand Rapids, MI*
3) Roberts	*8) "All Full of Tears and Flapdoodle"*
4) The Warriors	*9) Alice Paul*
5) Charles Taze Russell	*10) "MMMMMM," by Crash Test Dummies*

After giving the answers, find out how many questions people answered correctly. When it is established that everyone has failed the test miserably, grade the bonus question. If they answered "Jesus," they get an automatic perfect score. (If someone doesn't get the bonus question correct, you might need to sit down and have a talk with him!)

Comment, **"This test is an example of grace. Because you have faith that Jesus Christ is the Son of God, you get a perfect score on a test you could never come close to passing. Form groups of four and discuss grace, what it is and specific times you have received grace from God and other people."**

Allow them to discuss grace for a little while.

Then say, **"The world doesn't run on grace. It runs on performing and climbing and winning. What are some areas of your life where you are rewarded or punished based on your performance?"** (Allow for student response.) Ask them to discuss these questions in their groups:

- **What is the "American Dream" based on?**
- **How is God different from this?**

Check This . . .
Show the clip from *Indiana Jones and the Last Crusade* that begins at one hour and 50 minutes into the movie. In the scene, Indy must literally take a step of faith out into thin air.

Materials needed:
Bibles; reproducible student sheet on page 30 of this book; writing utensils

Check This . . .
Play the song "Never Gonna Be as Big as Jesus," by Audio Adrenaline, recorded on their album *Bloom*, or Newsboys' song "Real Good Thing," from their album *Going Public*.

27

- What would happen if you could earn God's favor only through living a good life?
- Can you accept that we can't earn God's favor?
- Do you believe that God loves you the same, no matter how much or how little you do?

In their groups have students read Matthew 20:1-16. Then ask for responses from anyone in your group to these questions:

- How does this parable illustrate grace?
- Why is it fair that everyone received the same pay?
- Do you ever get angry or jealous when "undeserving" people receive blessings?

COMPLETING THE RUN

HEAR THAT?

Watch the clip from *Field of Dreams* that begins at 10 minutes into the movie. In this segment, we see Kevin Costner get a strange message to build a baseball field in the middle of his corn crop. This flies in the face of reason, but he decides to follow his "call," no matter how crazy it is.

Form groups of three where students are sitting. Then, ask them to answer these questions together:

- How is this clip similar to what Abraham did in Genesis 12:1-5?
- Do other people usually understand and support steps of faith?

Conclude this activity by allowing students to personally examine God's "call" on their own lives. Comment, **"God tends to ask us to step farther and farther in faith, taking longer steps each time. What is the last step of faith God asked you to make and what happened?"** (Ask any willing students to share their experiences.)

- What is God asking you to do now?
- How do you know when God is telling you to go or to do something?
- Why doesn't God give us all the information in the beginning?
- What are some ways to get confirmation that you heard God correctly?

NO ONE ASKED

Hand out copies of the reproducible student sheet located on page 31 and ask students to fill it out. Give them five minutes or so to finish, and then ask them to break into groups of three. Ask them to read Romans 5:8 out loud, then answer these questions in their groups:

- Why did Christ die for us?
- Did he have to go to the cross?
- Did he know people would reject his gift?
- How do you think Jesus feels when people refuse to turn to him?
- Was it foolish for him to die for people who reject him?

Conclude this session by challenging students to **"Take a few minutes to discuss your parents. They are not perfect, but typically they have given up a lot in order to raise you. Why do they do that?"** Ask them:

- How can you show your appreciation?
- Would showing appreciation make things easier at home?

Materials needed:
TV; VCR; *Field of Dreams* video; Bibles

Check This . . .
A great song to close with is "I Can Hear You," by Carolyn Arends. It is the title song from the album by the same name.

Materials needed:
Bibles; reproducible student sheets on pages 31, 32 of this book; writing utensils

Check This . . .
Perform "Dog's Best Friend," from *Sanctified Skits, Vol. I*. In the skit, a boy's dog begins to talk and thank him for all of the things he has done without being asked to.

28   Lesson 3

Distribute copies of the reproducible student sheet titled "Exercising Your Freedom" that's found on page 32 of this book. Encourage your students to honestly deal with this week's challenge.

Check This . . .
Play All Star United's song "Beautiful Thing," from their self-titled debut release or Third Day's "Love Song," from their self-titled album.

(IMPOSSIBLE QUIZ)

Please answer the following questions to the best of your ability:

1) Who became king of Judah after Manasseh?

2) Who was chief of the Forestry Service under President Teddy Roosevelt?

3) What is Barbie's (the doll) last name?

4) What is the team name for James Martin High School?

5) What is the full name of the founder of the Jehovah's Witnesses?

6) Who wrote the screenplay for *Star Wars: The Empire Strikes Back*?

7) Which city buys the most cream of mushroom soup in the United States?

8) What is the title for chapter 25 of *The Adventures of Huckleberry Finn*?

9) Who became the head of the National American Women's Suffrage Association's Congressional Committee in 1912?

10) What is the only Top Ten single that doesn't have a vowel in its title?

Bonus Question: Who is the Son of God?

30   Lesson 3   ©1999 by The Standard Publishing Company. Permission is granted to reproduce this page for ministry purposes only—not for resale.

SACRIFICIAL Love

There are some people who made great sacrifices for you without your even asking them to do so. In the space provided below, list the things both your parents and Jesus have done out of love for you, expecting nothing in return.

Jesus:

Parents:

©1999 by The Standard Publishing Company. Permission is granted to reproduce this page for ministry purposes only—not for resale.

Exercising Your Freedom

"Now that faith has come, we are no longer under the supervision of the law."—Galatians 3:25

Since we are free from living under the law, why do we have to follow it? Why can't we simply do whatever we want?

Over the course of this week, fill in why, as a follower of Christ, you should observe the following commandments:

• speaking the truth (Ephesians 4:15)

• abstaining from sexual immorality (1 Thessalonians 4:3)

• spending time with God (Jeremiah 29:12, 13)

• tithing (Malachi 3:8-10)

• refraining from gossip (Proverbs 26:20-22)

• witnessing (Acts 1:8)

• observing the Lord's Supper (Acts 2:42; 20:7)

• caring for the poor (Deuteronomy 15:11)

• getting baptized (Acts 2:37-39)

• attending church (Hebrews 10:24, 25)

• avoiding drunkenness (Romans 13:13, 14)

32   Lesson 3   ©1999 by The Standard Publishing Company. Permission is granted to reproduce this page for ministry purposes only—not for resale.

UNSHACKLED

Once we become children of God, our lives should change so drastically that people immediately notice the transformation. Often, though, this is not the case. In fact, surveys show that Christians lead lives statistically similar to non-Christians in the areas of divorce, sexual promiscuity, dishonesty and pornography use. Teens need to know that being different, a new creation, means being distinguishable from the rest of the world.

The biggest challenge facing teens is to stay free of all the worldly influences around them that want to make them slaves. It is a strange phenomenon that man fights for freedom from oppression, then often trades that freedom for a different form of slavery. Christians do this when they return to old sin patterns or begin new ones. Paul begs believers not to do this. We are royalty, children of God, and should live like we believe it!

This session will give your students a clear picture of their heritage in Christ, that of royalty, and warn them that the only way they can lose their status is to personally choose to leave the palace and spend time in prison.

GETTING STOKED

1 DRESS ME UP

Have a huge pile of clothes mixed up on the floor. (You can pick up several items extremely cheap at a thrift store and either donate the clothes back or give them to needy people in your community or church. Another option is to ask your church for clothes which will be donated after the activity. You would save money by not having to purchase the clothes.)

After your students have arrived, give them two minutes to dig through the pile and find some new clothes to put on over the ones they already have on. When the two minutes are up, hold an impromptu fashion show for everyone to show off their "make-over." (Make sure to have some upbeat music playing and plenty of open space for each student to present their best "runway strut.") You may even want to vote for the "most fashionable" model and let him or her keep the ensemble as a prize.

After the fashion show, ask students:

- **How many shirts do you own?**

LESSON TEXT
Galatians 3:26–4:20

LESSON FOCUS
A growing Christian abandons the slavery that comes from following the world and seeks the freedom found in Jesus instead.

LESSON GOALS
As a result of participating in this lesson, students will:

- Discover that all Christians are children of God.
- Realize that non-Christians are slaves of the world.
- Choose to escape from slavery.
- Commit themselves to building a strong foundation.

Materials needed:
Lots of secondhand clothes; Bibles

Check This . . .
A great song to play during the fashion show is "Dress Me Up," recorded by Eric Champion on his *Transformation* album.

33

Check This . . .
Play one of two video clips from
Clueless (PG-13). The first one begins
at 11 minutes into the movie and shows
Alicia Silverstone picking out what
clothes to wear in the morning. The second begins at 36 minutes and shows
Alicia giving her friend a complete make-
over.

Materials needed:
"Hello! My name is . . ." stickers; Bibles

Check This . . .
Play one of the following songs to enliven
your discussion on how Christians
should respond to racism: "Colored
People," from dc Talk's *Jesus Freak*
album; "Skin," from Speck's self-titled
album; or "Let's Face It," by the secular
group The Mighty Mighty Bosstones,
recorded on their *Let's Face It* album.

Materials needed:
Amistad video; VCR; TV; Bibles

• **How many pairs of pants?**
• **How many pairs of shoes?**

Comment, **"You constantly change clothes. Each of you has several different
outfits for school, work, church, hanging out, dates, sports, etc. Each one of
you has an outfit that you may not have used yet. Please read Galatians
3:26–4:20."** Allow time for them to read. Then ask them the following questions:

• **What does being clothed in Christ mean in verse 27?**
• **How do you take off your own nature and put on Christ?**
• **Do people see Jesus when they see you?**

COMMON DENOMINATOR

As your students are arriving, distribute "Hello! My name is . . ." stickers that you have already labeled with descriptions like "father,"
"Asian," "firefighter," "student" and "African." Give every student a different label
to wear as everyone wanders around the room, meeting people and trying to figure out what they all share in common. After five minutes or so, bring the group
back together. Ask them to state what they all share in common. The answer is
that they are all part of the human race. (Share this answer with them if they do
not guess it.) Break them into small groups of three or four (perhaps by the different labels they are wearing) to answer the following questions:

• **If we are all from the human race, why is there a problem with prejudice
  and racism?**
• **Are you prejudiced toward a particular group of people? Why or why not?**

Ask groups to read Galatians 3:26–4:9 out loud within their groups. Then, allow
them to grapple with these questions:

• **Does God see race? What does he look at?**
• **How should a Christian respond to racism?**
• **Why do we have more reason than non-Christians to be color-blind?**
• **How does our youth group as a whole treat people who are racially differ-
  ent from us?**
• **Can we do anything to improve?**

Allow time for a brief brainstorming session with your group on how racial bar-
riers can be torn down in your ministry, schools and city. Seek out ways your
ministry can build bridges to believers who might look different on the outside, but
who serve the same Lord.

DROPPING IN

NEVER GOIN' BACK AGAIN

In order to give your students a taste of how horrible slavery is, show a
clip from the Steven Spielberg film *Amistad* (rated R for violence). The
opening clip shows exactly how desperate a man can be to gain his freedom. (Stop
the scene before the battle.) This shocking scene details the nightmare of being
transported as a slave across the ocean. Try to find some acceptable portions to
show your youth group to help them visualize spiritual slavery to sin.

After your students have viewed the video clip, say, **"Slavery is a horrible
thing. Have you ever felt like you were a slave to something?"** Ask for responses to this question:

34   Lesson 4

• **How does the clip we saw relate to life without Jesus Christ?**

Ask students to reread Galatians 4:8, 9. Then discuss these questions:

• **How does sin make us a slave?**

• **Can we be forced into slavery?**

• **What does it mean to be a slave to the world?**

• **What can we do to help others escape their slavery?**

• **How do you know if you are a slave or not?**

• **Why would you turn back to a life of slavery?**

Ask them to reread Galatians 4:1, 2 and discuss what it means, by dealing with these questions:

• **If Christ has set us free, why do we still have to answer to an authority other than ourselves?**

• **Who is the guardian and trustee of your life?**

Comment, **"In Luke 11:23, Jesus says that we are either for him or against him. This means you either choose to be a slave to Jesus, or Satan chooses you to be his slave. Do you believe this?"** Conclude this activity by asking:

• **How does being a slave to God actually grant you freedom?**

• **What are the benefits of serving God instead of being a slave to the world?**

WE ARE FAMILY

Find someone (preferably one of your students) who is adopted to come to your meeting and briefly share from his or her experience exactly what it means to be legally adopted. This person should tell how it felt before and after being chosen by a family to become their son or daughter. After the speaker finishes sharing, ask your students to break into small groups and discuss these questions:

• **How would it feel to not know who your biological parents were?**

• **How do you think people who don't know God feel?**

If anyone in the group recently became a Christian, you might let her share a brief testimony of her life before being adopted into the family of Christ and the change in her life since the conversion. Ask everyone to read 2 Thessalonians 2:13 to themselves.

Comment, **"Close your eyes and think back to elementary school when people would pick teams for a game. How did you feel waiting to be chosen?"**

• **How did it feel to be chosen?**

• **Did you know that God chose you?**

• **How does that make you feel?**

Distribute copies of the student sheet located on page 38 of this book. Allow students time to complete it. You can serve as witness, or if possible, ask a church member who is a Notary Public to come to your meeting to seal each adoption certificate, making them "legal" adoption papers.

Check This . . .
Some songs that deal with this choice between slavery to sin or to God include: All Star United's "Torn," from their self-titled release; Skillet's "Promise Blender," from their self-titled album; and Dime Store Prophets' "Soothsayer Speaks," from their album *Fantastic Distraction*.

Materials needed:
Bibles; reproducible student sheet on page 38 of this book; writing utensils

Check This . . .
Play the scene from *Benny & Joon* which begins at 49 minutes into the movie. It shows where Benny and Joon's parents die and they are orphaned. The video clip will enable your students to visualize life without any parents.

35

COMPLETING THE RUN

READING OF THE WILL

Materials needed:
Envelopes; wills; bequeathed items; reproducible student sheet on page 39 of this book; writing utensils

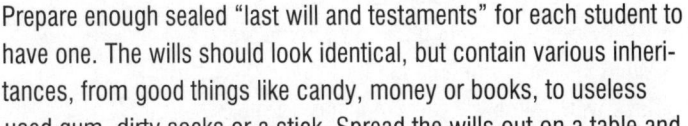

Prepare enough sealed "last will and testaments" for each student to have one. The wills should look identical, but contain various inheritances, from good things like candy, money or books, to useless things like used gum, dirty socks or a stick. Spread the wills out on a table and invite each student to come forward and choose one. While students are choosing their envelopes, explain the following:

"A wealthy great aunt you never knew recently died and left you an inheritance. In your hand is her last will and testament that tells you what you received. One at a time, come forward and I will read the will and you will receive whatever your great aunt left you."

Have the students come forward in an orderly fashion and give you their great aunt's will. When you read each bequeathal, have one of your adult leaders bring out the item and present it to the student. After all of the wills have been read, ask:

- **How did you feel while waiting for the will to be read?**
- **How did you feel after you found out what you were to receive?**
- **Did any of you deserve the inheritance you received?**
- **How is this similar to the inheritance you have waiting in Heaven?**
- **Why do we receive an inheritance from God?**

Distribute copies of the reproducible student sheet located on page 39 and ask the students to work on them in groups of five.

MOM'S RIGHT THERE!

Materials needed:
Bibles; reproducible student sheet on page 40 of this book

To begin this activity, break your students into groups of four, asking them to choose from among these four options as their favorite family vacation activity: going to the beach, camping, skiing or going to an amusement park.

Once they have gathered in their "vacation spot" groups, say, **"Share with each other a time when you were extremely embarrassed because your parents were with you when something happened. This should be something that wouldn't bother you normally, like a movie or a joke, but made you feel uncomfortable because your parents were with you."**

Allow a few minutes for discussion before presenting the next situation to discuss.

"Think back over the last week and tell your group a time you would have been embarrassed if your parents had been with you."

After sufficient time, ask them to reread Galatians 4:6.

Comment, **"According to this verse, we have the Spirit of God, the Holy Spirit, living inside us. That means God is with us every second of every hour of every day, going everywhere you go and witnessing everything you do. Should you act any differently since God is always in the room?"**

Ask them to take turns carefully reading John 14:15-31 and 16:5-16 out loud in their groups. Then they can answer these questions:

- **Why is the Holy Spirit in us?**
- **Why did Jesus say it is better for us to have the Holy Spirit here than**

36 Lesson 4

for him to stay?

- **What is the Holy Spirit supposed to do?**
- **Do you believe the Holy Spirit is active in your life? Why or why not?**
- **What can keep the Holy Spirit from actively impacting your life?**
- **What can you do to allow the Holy Spirit to be more active in your daily life?**

Close with a time of prayer asking for greater sensitivity to the Holy Spirit during the week and a renewed willingness to let him work in their lives. Then distribute copies of the reproducible student sheet titled "Exercising Your Freedom" that's found on page 40 of this book.

Check This . . .
Play Third Day's song "Consuming Fire," from their self-titled album.

Official Adoption Certificate

Let it be known that _____ is a child of Yahweh, Almighty God, Creator of the universe. This adoption gives _____ all of the rights and privileges of a member of Jehovah's family: an inheritance in Heaven, constant access to the throne of God, 24-hour protection provided by the Army of God, and purification from all sin.

I hereby certify that this certificate was presented in _____ county of _____ (state) this _____ day of _____ (month) in the year _____.

Signature _____

Witness _____

38   Lesson 4   ©1999 by The Standard Publishing Company. Permission is granted to reproduce this page for ministry purposes only—not for resale.

Eternal Inheritance

Did you know you have an inheritance waiting for you in Heaven? There won't be a funeral to attend or a lawyer to read a will. This inheritance will last for eternity and be given to you by Jesus Christ himself. In fact, he is preparing it for you right now! Look up the Scripture verses below and list beside them anything that you will receive or experience as part of your inheritance in Heaven.

Revelation 21:1–22:6

John 14:2, 3

1 Corinthians 15:35-44

Remember, by serving Christ today on earth, these and many other heavenly gifts are being stored up for you in Heaven for later.

©1999 by The Standard Publishing Company. Permission is granted to reproduce this page for ministry purposes only—not for resale.

Exercising Your Freedom

zeal *n.* ardor for a person, cause or object; eager desire or endeavor; enthusiastic diligence

Everyone is full of zeal (zealous) for something in his or her life. The definition above should describe your passion for Jesus Christ and his kingdom. As a royal heir, free from slavery to the world (Galatians 4:7), you should live in confidence and zeal (2 Timothy 1:7).

Cut out the figure and the "clothes" below. Tape the body next to your mirror and dress it each evening this week according to how you lived your day. Did you live like a royal heir of God (robe), or a slave to the world (sackcloth), or simply coast through the day (jump suit)? When you see the figure in the morning, remember that you are royalty and should live the day in such a way that you can put on your royal robe at night, having lived the day zealously for your Father and Lord (Galatians 3:26, 27).

40   Lesson 4   ©1999 by The Standard Publishing Company. Permission is granted to reproduce this page for ministry purposes only—not for resale.

KICKIN' IT LIVE

Every student leader and parent knows that teens face intense peer pressure every day. (Many of us still experience it at work!) Friends, classmates, even teachers push and pull your kids in every different direction, encouraging, cajoling, sometimes even threatening them to say, do and become things they would never consider doing if left alone.

Your students also experience peer pressure at church. This can be pressure to dress, talk or think exactly like the rest of the church body, creating an army of clones made not necessarily in a pleasing image of what God wants, but into an image of what we *think* pleases God. The early church faced this problem when it came to circumcision. (Have fun discussing that one with your group!) Many early Christians believed God accepted as his children only those who performed this outward symbol. Paul disagreed vehemently, warning that a man who attempts to justify himself before God based on performance cannot do so by following only part of the Law, but instead must keep every bit of the entire thing. Only Christ's grace-giving death on the cross saves us from condemnation. We can never work our way into Heaven.

This session should reinforce the fact that we are free in Christ, not bound by outward rules and regulations. All Christ requires of us is to love him and everyone around us. (No problem, right?)

GETTING STOKED

THE BIRDBRAINS OF ALCATRAZ

When the students arrive, inform them that they are all part of a jail-break from Alcatraz Penitentiary. They must swim across the ocean to the mainland (a span of fifteen feet) quickly or the guards will wake up and catch them. The only problem is the water is infested with great white sharks so fierce they make Jaws look like a Teletubbie™. Luckily, each group has one "shark repellent suit." They must get everyone across the water using whatever method they want. The catch is each person can wear the "suit" only ONCE. If the student wears it across the water, he or she cannot wear it again. Only the one person in the "shark repellent suit" may be in the water (i.e., touching the floor) at a time. If anyone other than the person wearing the suit touches the water

---

LESSON TEXT
Galatians 5:1-6, 13-26

LESSON FOCUS
Christ has freed us from slavish lawkeeping and uncontrolled lawlessness to loving service.

LESSON GOALS
As a result of participating in this lesson, students will:

- Express appreciation to God for their freedom from the Law.
- Discover that freedom doesn't mean a license to sin.
- Commit to loving God and loving their neighbors as themselves.

Materials needed:
Bibles; some kind of clothing for the "shark repellent suits"

Check This . . .
You might begin by showing the final scene in *The Truman Show* where Jim Carrey refuses to conform to what everyone is telling him to do and instead breaks out of his "prison."

41

Check This . . .
During the game, play clips from *The Fugitive* (PG-13) where Harrison Ford is escaping (running from the train, jumping from the dam, etc.) or the shark from *Jaws*. You could also play the soundtrack from either film as background music.

(ground), he or she is immediately devoured by the sharks.

If possible, form groups of between fifteen and twenty students. Even better, have your entire group work together, since this can serve as a team builder as well as an object lesson. Let every team finish the task, with the groups who finish first cheering the others on. Give the team who finishes first a prize of some sort if you want.

Once the game is over, have your students come back together in one large group. Say: **"You were pretending to escape from prison. Have any of you ever been physically trapped or locked up some place you wanted to leave?"** Give students a chance to share their experiences and how they felt when trapped.

Ask, **"How did it feel to be set free?"** Allow the same students to share their feelings.

Ask, **"Were any of you set free from sin or misery when you accepted Christ?"** Allow a few more students to share their testimonies. After everyone is finished, break into groups of three. Have them take turns reading verses from Galatians 5:1-6, 13-26 out loud.

Conclude this activity by saying, **"So many times we trade in our freedom for a prison we make ourselves. Let's see what God wants for our lives and what he wants us to do in order to stay free."**

Materials needed:
Indiana Jones and the Last Crusade video; VCR; TV; Bibles

JAILBREAK

Show the clip from *Indiana Jones and the Last Crusade* where Indy and his father escape from the German military installation. It begins at one hour and one minute into the movie. Stop the clip before the Joneses escape on a motorcycle. (You may want to stop it sooner. Play enough to get across the point that our heroes are escaping from a prison.)

After playing the film clip, ask, **"Do you think Indy and his dad would ever break back into the Nazi base, tie themselves up and wait to be executed?"**

Wait for their obvious "No" response, then comment, **"Many of us spend our whole lives trying to escape a situation only to later put ourselves right back in the same situation. When we commit to Christ, we escape living under the law. Sometimes we make life difficult, though, by assuming our burdens again even though we don't have to. Let's see what Paul says about freedom and how to keep it."**

Have your students take turns reading aloud from Galatians 5:1-6, 13-26.

DROPPING IN

WON'T YOU BE MY NEIGHBOR?

Materials needed:
Butcher paper; telephone book; Bibles; markers; world map transparency; overhead projector; reproducible student sheet on page 46 of this book; writing utensils

Hang a large sheet of blank butcher paper on the wall with "Galatians 5:14" written across the top in bold letters. Say, **"Paul pleads with the Galatians here to accept the freedom Christ offers and not to try to keep a list of 'do's and don'ts.'"**

Ask students these questions;
• **Why does Satan try to get us to concentrate on the do's and don'ts?**
• **Are there controversies in the church today similar to the circumcision debate in Paul's time?**

Allow time for discussion, then read Galatians 5:14 out loud together. After

42 Lesson 5

everyone reads the verse together in unison, say, **"This verse is the key to free-dom in Christ."**

Break everyone into groups of four. Tear out pages from the telephone book and distribute one page to each group. Ask them to write a list of people they consider to be their neighbors on the page with their markers. Give them a few minutes to complete their lists, then gather up the lists. While you compile their answers into a master list on the butcher paper, have them answer the questions on the reproducible student sheet on page 46.

When everyone completes the student sheet, ask:

- **Do you always treat others as well as you treat yourself? Why not?**
- **Does anyone want to add a new name to our list?**

Add any new names your students suggest to the butcher paper list.

Ask, **"Why didn't you consider these people neighbors when you made your first list?"** Allow people who added new names to explain. After everyone is satisfied with the list, project a transparency of a world map onto the butcher paper so it covers the list of names.

Comment, **"The entire world is your neighbor. We are all sinners in need of God's perfect salvation, and as Christians we are called to love everyone. That means you're supposed to try to see every single person the way God does: with love and compassion. This is extremely hard to do, but that doesn't mean we shouldn't try."** Ask students these questions:

- **How does loving God and our neighbors keep us from becoming imprisoned?**
- **What are some ways you can love God more?**
- **What are some ways you can love your neighbors more?**

Allow your group to brainstorm ways in which your youth ministry can demonstrate love to others. This could be as simple as sitting with a visitor to as elaborate as organizing a mission trip. Vote on one idea and encourage everyone in the group to focus on that one love demonstration for the next few weeks.

STUPID HUMAN TRICKS

Ask your students to spread out around the room. Make sure there is plenty of space between each of them so that no one gets hit inadvertently when they start moving. Once everyone has enough personal space, explain that you are going to give them different physical challenges and that they need to do their best to conquer each one. The challenges consist of several different contortions that most people find very difficult to perform. (Be sure to stress that they SHOULD NOT hurt themselves trying to do these!) The different tasks are:

- **Touch your tongue to your nose.**
- **Touch the fingers of your right hand to your right forearm.**
- **Clasp your hands together behind your back and bring them in front of you without letting go of your hands.**
- **Touch your foot to your nose.**
- **Put your leg behind your head.**

(You can add any others that you can think of.)

Allow a minute or two of "struggle" for each physical challenge. (Reward any people who actually can do what you ask with prizes if you want to, or have a "freak show" at the end with all of the winners showing off their "talents.") Once

Check This . . .
Songs which underscore God's definition of "neighbor" include: "Hey You, I Love Your Soul," from Skillet's *Hey You, I Love Your Soul* album; "Broadway," from Sherri Youngward's *Faces Memories Places* album; and "Empath," from The Echoing Green's self-titled release.

Materials needed:
Slips of paper; writing utensils; Bibles; shoe box

43

everyone is seated (and has all their limbs back in place), ask:

- **How many of you found those things difficult?**
- **Why were they hard?**

Comment, **"You were all fighting with your body in the physical sense just now, trying to get it to do something it did not want to do. Let's read how this can happen to us spiritually."**

Break everyone into groups of three and have them read a verse each from Galatians 5:16-18 within their groups. Then ask them to discuss these questions:

- **How many of you can relate to these verses?**
- **Does freedom in Christ give us a license to do whatever we want? Why or why not?**
- **What's the point in trying to live without sin if God is going to forgive you when you ask him to?** Allow this bomb to settle. Keep the discussion focused as they battle over this one.

Comment, **"This passage basically says that when we identify with Christ, we are no longer slaves to sin. If that is true, why do we continue to struggle with sin when Christ's death conquered sin?"** Once again, open up the floor for discussion.

Pass out slips of paper and have your students write down a sin they constantly struggle with. Bring out a jail you have made beforehand using a shoe box (be as creative as you want with bars or barbed wire or even guards decorating the box!) and have everyone drop their sins into "jail."

Then say something like, **"Christ's sacrifice on the cross has placed our sins in jail. We're the only ones who can open the door and let sin rule over our lives again."** Allow group discussion of the following questions:

- **Why would someone choose to return to sin?**
- **What are some steps you can take to avoid falling into the sin you just put into jail?**
- **How will concentrating on loving God and others keep you from sinning?**

Throw away the box to symbolize your students' freedom from those sins. If you can, an even more effective display is to set the box on fire so your students can watch their sins burn away in Christ's holy flame. (Just make sure there's a fire extinguisher on hand!)

COMPLETING THE RUN

UNCHAINED

Get a chain (something simple from a bicycle, keychain or wallet will do). Break the chain into individual links before the meeting starts. Give a broken link from the chain to each student at this time.

Comment, **"This piece of chain symbolizes the chain that bound you before Christ set you free. Keep this broken piece of chain in your pocket this week to remind yourself that following Christ breaks the chains of Satan and the condemnation of the Law, sets you free from sin and gives you life abundant. Every time you feel this in your pocket, remember to love God and others."**

Have your group break into pairs to pray for the strength to love others during the week. Also, challenge them to memorize Galatians 5:14 for next week.

Check This . . .
Two songs that deal with the focus of this activity are Jeni Varnadeau's "Why Would You Go Back," from her *Colors of Truth* album and Creed's "My Own Prison," from their secular album of the same title. Play the song while students fill out their papers.

Materials needed:
A chain

Check This . . .
Play the song "Cry for Freedom," from Rich Mullins' musical *Canticle of the Plains*.

---

44 Lesson 5

LOVING THE UNLOVABLE

Begin by saying, **"It is easy to talk about loving God and others, but a little more difficult to actually put it into practice. Why is it so hard to love other people?"**

Pass out the reproducible student sheet on page 47 and have your students break into pairs while filling it out.

Ask, **"What does God want us to do when we really can't stand someone?"** Allow time for the groups to discuss. Then ask students to answer these questions:

- **Why does Galatians 5:14 sum up the entire law?**
- **How does loving each other prevent you from sinning personally?**

Have the pairs pray for each other as they try to love the person they wrote down on their paper. Challenge them to memorize either Galatians 5:14 or 1 John 4:19 as a reminder of their commitment to love the people around them.

As students are dismissed, distribute copies of the reproducible student sheet titled "Exercising Your Freedom" that's found on page 48 of this book. This week your students will be focusing on the fruit of the Spirit.

Materials needed:
Reproducible student sheets on page 47, 48 of this book; writing utensils

Check This . . .
Play Michael W. Smith's song "Love One Another," from his *Change Your World* album; or, conclude on a lighter but still meaningful note with VeggieTales' song "Love Your Neighbor," from their *Veggie Tunes* album.

45

What would YOU do?

What would you do for yourself if you were in the following situations?

- If you were cold?

- If you were dying of thirst?

- If you were sleeping on the street?

- If your car were broken down on the side of the road?

- If your shoes had holes in them?

- If you were mad at someone?

- If you were trying to change lanes on a busy highway?

- If you had not eaten all day?

- If you did not know the gospel?

- If you were addicted to drugs or alcohol?

Look at the list you have just made of things you would do out of love for yourself. Remember that Christ has called you to do these exact same things for your neighbors. Jesus defines your neighbor as anyone you meet who has a need. (See the parable of the Good Samaritan in Luke 10:25-37.)

46   Lesson 5   ©1999 by The Standard Publishing Company. Permission is granted to reproduce this page for ministry purposes only—not for resale.

Thorn in Your Side

"We love because he first loved us." —1 John 4:19

God calls us to love everyone. Often this is easier said than done. What about that jerk in math class? What about that jealous girl who always shoots you dirty looks? Those are the people we should love. Thankfully, God gives us the ability to love the unlovable (1 John 4:7). Think about that while answering the questions below.

The person I have the hardest time loving is . . .

The thing that bugs me most about him (her) is . . .

I will pray that God will help him (her) in . . .

I will pray that God will help me . . .

I should love _____ because . . .

What can I do this week to demonstrate my love for _____?

Exercising Your Freedom

Every child of God receives the fruit of the Spirit (Galatians 5:22, 23); it's just up to you whether it is allowed to grow or not. Look up the definition for each day's fruit and write it below. Pray that God will provide situations that day for you to live out each trait. When you come home each day, recount below your success or failure in exhibiting that particular fruit of the Spirit.

		Definition	How I did today
Day 1	Love		
Day 2	Joy		
Day 3	Peace		
Day 4	Patience/ gentleness		
Day 5	Kindness/ goodness		
Day 6	Faithfulness		
Day 7	Self-control		

48   **Lesson 5**   ©1999 by The Standard Publishing Company. Permission is granted to reproduce this page for ministry purposes only—not for resale.

FREE RIDE

Now comes the hardest part—application. Your students have perfected the art of cramming. They can memorize the periodic table in three hours, take a test on it, and completely forget it three minutes after they hand their papers in. The Christian life isn't like school, though. God's lessons are meant to stick in the brain for a lifetime. Even harder than remembering what God teaches is the fact that we are supposed to actually take those words to heart and live them every day.

Paul lists several commands and admonitions in chapter six of Galatians. The easiest one for your students to understand and try to put into action is also the hardest to achieve in everyday interaction with the world—doing good to all people. They are taught by everything and everyone around them to get revenge or even destroy people who get in their way or "offend" them in some way. Christ preaches a very different message to the world—love your enemies and show kindness to those who try to hurt you.

This session should remind your students that their freedom in Christ brings with it the responsibility of treating other people as Christ would, no matter what their personal feelings about the person are.

GETTING STOKED

TIRED?

Ask all of your students to sit in their chairs and then raise their feet up off the floor until their legs are parallel to the floor. Their legs and feet should be supported by nothing but their leg and stomach muscles. Have them hold this position for two minutes if they can. Bring any people who accomplish this feat to the front for a direct battle to see who can hold their legs out straight for the longest time possible. Reward the winner with a soft drink or some other prize.

After every foot is back on the floor, break your students into groups of three. Say, **"I wanted you to experience what it means to be weary. Share with your group a time when you were the most completely bone-dead tired of your life."**

After they finish sharing stories, have each group read Galatians 6:1-10, 14 out loud, focusing on Galatians 6:9. Then ask students to discuss these questions in their groups:

LESSON TEXT
Galatians 6:1-10, 14

LESSON FOCUS
Those who have truly experienced freedom in Jesus will treat other people as he would.

LESSON GOALS
As a result of participating in this lesson, students will:
- Be able to discern between burdens and loads.
- Demonstrate an attitude of humility.
- Commit to doing good to all people.

Materials needed:
Prize; Bibles

Check This . . .
Play the secular group Smash Mouth's song, "Why Can't We Be Friends," from their *Fush Yu Mang* album.

49

- Do you ever tire of doing good? Why or why not?
- Why should we do good to a person who treats us badly?
- What is the nicest thing someone has ever done for you?
- Do you think Jesus was ever tempted to *not* do good?

Ask your students to close their eyes and think of a person who makes them "weary," someone who totally gets on their nerves. Ask them to replay in their minds the last time they had contact with that person. Now they should rewind the scene, but this time they should do good to the annoying person.

Ask, **"Did the scene change? Try to do good to that person the next time you see him or her and discover what good can do."**

LEVEL PLAYING FIELD

Ask everyone to find a partner and spread out around the room.

Explain: **"Take the next few minutes to describe your hero to your partner. This can be someone you know, someone famous or even an historical figure. Describe why you admire the person and what you want to copy from his or her life."**

After both partners have described their heroes, present the opposite scenario.

"This time, I want you to describe the person you despise most. You may know him or her, or have heard about him or her in the news or read about him or her in history. Name the trait you most hate about this person and why you would never want to be like him or her."

When everyone has had time to talk, ask the group to read Galatians 6:1-10, 14, concentrating on Galatians 6:9, 10. Then ask students to answer these questions in pairs:

- **To whom are we to do good?**
- **What does this mean for the people you just described?**
- **Why does God command us to do good?**
- **How does God see the people you described?**
- **What can you do to see people through God's eyes of love?**

Encourage the partners to pray with each other for God's help in viewing people the way he does and doing good to every person they meet.

DROPPING IN

CARRY THAT WEIGHT

Get each student to donate an item to you (a watch, shoe, gum, wallet, anything). Pile all of the items together on one side of the room. Give each student an opportunity to carry everything in the pile across the room in one trip. (If you have either a small group or only pocket-sized items donated, be sure to place something large in the pile to ensure the feat cannot be accomplished.) Once everyone attempts (unsuccessfully) to carry everyone's "burdens," let them retrieve their possessions from the pile and sit down in groups of three to five. Pass out markers and brown paper grocery sacks.

Comment, **"Please read Galatians 6:1-5 again. Define 'load' and 'burden' using those verses and write them on your grocery sack. Turn it in to me when you finish."**

Compile of list of student responses on a sheet of butcher paper or a chalk-

Materials needed:
Bibles

Check This . . .
Play Dime Store Prophet's song "Hitler's Girlfriend," from their *Love Is Against the Grain* album.

Materials needed:
Bibles; paper grocery sacks; markers; butcher paper or chalk and chalkboard

50   Lesson 6

board. Once you have all of the definitions, read them out loud and brainstorm definitions for the words with the entire group. When everyone is generally satisfied, ask:

- **Why should we help with "burdens," but leave "loads" alone?**
- **Why do we compare ourselves with others?**
- **How can someone else's burden tempt you?**
- **Can a "load" turn into a "burden" or vice versa?**

Next, ask each group to concentrate on Galatians 6:3. Then discuss these questions:

- **What does this verse mean exactly?**
- **Can you never feel good about serving God?**
- **How can you keep perspective on your spiritual "deeds"?**
- **Can you honestly check yourself, or do you need help to arrive at an accurate self-evaluation?**

Allow a few minutes for the groups to pray with one another about their burdens and loads.

HUMBLE THYSELF

Distribute the slips of paper and say, **"Please write down the first thing that comes to your mind when I say the word 'humble.'"**

Gather up the answers and read them out loud to the entire group. Divide students into groups of three or four and say, **"God sees humility and serving others a little differently than we do. With your group, fill out the answers on the sheet I'm handing out to better understand God's view."**

Allow approximately ten minutes for them to complete the reproducible sheet. Then ask for answers to these questions:

- **Why does God desire for us to be humble?**
- **Is it wrong to be confident?**
- **What is the difference between confidence and arrogance?**
- **Can you be too humble?**

Comment, **"The best example of being a servant was exemplified by Jesus in John 13 when he washed his disciples' feet. In Jesus' day, washing someone's feet was a job reserved only for slaves or the lowest house servant. A person of higher social standing NEVER washed the feet of someone below him in society. Jesus, the Master, turned this belief on its head by washing his followers' feet. We should all follow Christ's example by serving other people."**

Give these instructions to your students: **"I would like all of you to take off your shoes and socks so I can wash your feet. I hope that by doing this you will be humbled and desire to do the same for the people in your life."**

Either have the students come forward to you, or go to them with a bowl of water and a towel to wash their feet. If you have too many students, ask some of your adult leaders to join in and help you.

Check This . . .
Play the Beatles' song "Carry That Weight," from their *Abbey Road* album or "Hope to Carry On," from either Rich Mullins on his *Never Picture Perfect* album or the self-titled release from Caedmon's Call.

Materials needed:
Slips of paper; writing utensils; reproducible student sheet on page 54 of this book; towels; basin of water

Check This . . .
During the foot-washing experience, some nice background music would be Rich Mullins' song "You Did Not Have a Home," from his album *The Jesus Record*.

51

COMPLETING THE RUN

WHO'S THE TEACHER?

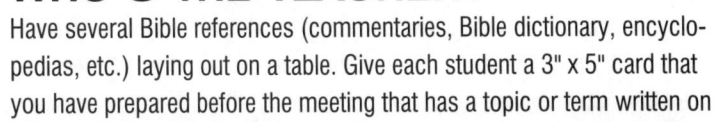

Have several Bible references (commentaries, Bible dictionary, encyclopedias, etc.) laying out on a table. Give each student a 3" x 5" card that you have prepared before the meeting that has a topic or term written on it such as Antioch, cubit or Cyrus. Give your students five minutes to use the reference books to discover all they can about their assigned subjects, writing the most important facts down on the index cards.

When the five minutes are up, allow each student to share briefly what he or she has learned with the group. (If time does not allow for this, have students turn to the person next to them and share.) When everyone finishes reporting, ask students to form groups of four and read Galatians 6:6 out loud. Then, have them discuss these questions in their groups:

- **Do you learn about the Bible only from pastors?**
- **Where else can you learn biblical truths?**
- **Why does God command us to share our knowledge with each other?**
- **Do you regularly share what God teaches you? Why or why not?**

Ask everyone to partner with the person next to them. Inform them that next week they will have a few minutes to share with their partners what God taught them during the week. They don't have to give detailed reports; they just need to get in the habit of telling someone else about the new things that God teaches them.

THE UNBREAKABLE BOND

Split the group in half. Hand out Styrofoam cups to each student. One group will receive cups filled with fast-acting cement (dry), and the other group a cup filled with water and a popsicle stick (or something else sturdy that they can stir with). Match partners from each group to combine the contents of their cups, stirring to create cement. After a few minutes of hardening, ask everyone to be seated. Then ask:

- **What happened when you combined the two cups' ingredients?**
- **Could you build a house on the ingredients when they are separate?**
- **What happens when believers come together and build each other up?**
- **How is encouragement like quick-drying cement?**

Comment, **"Galatians 6 shows us we need one another. Right now, we are going to choose someone to be our encourager for the week. The only words that should come out of your mouth to this partner next week should be encouraging ones."**

Help everyone find partners and distribute copies of the reproducible student sheet located on page 55 of this book. Give students plenty of time to talk and exchange completed sheets. Have partners close in prayer for one another before they leave.

After the discussion ends, ask your students to consider getting an accountability partner. Say, **"We all need someone whom we can trust and open up to, sharing our victories and defeats, becoming a source of encouragement during our journey toward becoming like Christ. This partnership is similar to a lawyer's and his clients—nothing that is shared is passed on to anyone else. Seriously consider finding someone to be your accountability partner in the**

Materials needed:
Bible reference materials; 3" x 5" index cards; Bibles; writing utensils

Check This . . .
Play the song "Going Public," from Newsboys' *Going Public* album.

Materials needed:
Styrofoam cups; water; quick-drying cement; popsicle sticks; reproducible student sheets on pages 55, 56 of this book; writing utensils

Check This . . .
Play Jars of Clay's song "Flood," from their self-titled release, or Michael W. Smith's song "Pray for Me," from his *i (2) Eye* album.

52   Lesson 6

next month or so. It will help you immensely in your Christian walk."

As students are dismissed, distribute copies of the reproducible student sheet titled "Exercising Your Freedom" that's found on page 56 of this book. Encourage students to take the kindness challenge this week.

HUMBLE THYSELF

Read Galatians 6:4.
• Why shouldn't you compare yourself to others?

• Does God ever compare you with others?

• Why does comparison with others crush humility?

Read Galatians 6:14.
• Why do we boast in our abilities and accomplishments?

• Who gave us those talents?

• Can you lose those gifts?

• Why would we boast in something given to us?

Read Galatians 6:2.
• How are we to serve others?

• Are there any jobs too lowly for a Christian to perform?

• Is there any person we should not humbly serve? Why or why not?

54   Lesson 6   ©1999 by The Standard Publishing Company. Permission is granted to reproduce this page for ministry purposes only—not for resale.

PUMP YOU UP

When is the last time you were encouraged by someone? Was it at church, home, work or school?

We live in a society filled with put-downs. That is why you are going to be a pick-me-up this week. Find a partner, fill out your responses below and exchange sheets. Then, pray for each other and contact each other at least every other day next week. Your purpose is to build each other up, speaking only positive words of encouragement (Galatians 6:10).

Name _____

Birthday _____

Address _____

Phone number _____

Favorite hobby

Favorite Scripture verse

A situation that is discouraging me

A person who puts me down

The place I am most discouraged

Some of my prayer requests

A problem I'm having at school or home

©1999 by The Standard Publishing Company. Permission is granted to reproduce this page for ministry purposes only—not for resale.

55

Exercising Your Freedom

Choose two people, a Christian and a non-Christian, to whom you can do good this week. Below is a journal to record entries concerning the kindness you show each person. You may want to pick people you do not normally get along with or even like very much so you can see the difference your kindness makes in your relationship with that person.

Each day, come home and write the "good" things you do for each person. In a different color ink, write any kind things they do for you. At the end of the week, note any change in their attitude toward you. Be sure to look for any opportunities to display God's love. (This can be as simple as smiling and saying hello to them, giving them a ride home or listening to their problems.) Also be sure to pray specifically for each person every day. Commit to showing them kindness, even if they show you none in return.

NAME: (Christian)	NAME: (Non-Christian)
Monday	Monday
Tuesday	Tuesday
Wednesday	Wednesday
Thursday	Thursday
Friday	Friday
Saturday	Saturday
Sunday	Sunday
Changes	Changes

56   Lesson 6   ©1999 by The Standard Publishing Company. Permission is granted to reproduce this page for ministry purposes only—not for resale.

ESCAPE FROM ALBADONIA

THE BACKGROUND

Our story is set before the Europeans came to America in the ancient city of Albadonia, the largest, wealthiest, most progressive city in the Western Hemisphere. Unfortunately, Niko the Terrible rules the metropolis with an iron fist, subjecting the city's commoners to inhuman working conditions and constant fear of arrest and torture. Niko keeps the people in their place with his ruthless Royal Guard, an elite fighting force who terrorize the citizens and imprison them on a whim.

Hope for the oppressed people comes from Elysia. A few fortunate people fled the city and created a community where fulfilling, abundant life and freedom rule, not the evil dictator Niko. Finding Elysia is difficult and dangerous, though. Niko's hatred for the hidden city burns brighter than the sun and he freely tortures or martyrs any Elysian he catches in the hopes of finding and destroying their city. Those caught attempting to leave Albadonia receive a life sentence in prison. Freedom does not come easily to those seeking it.

THE PURPOSE

This event is designed both as a fun celebration for your students after finishing the study and as an outreach for their friends. Announce this event at least three weeks in advance. You may want to start hyping it from the first session of this book. Explain to your students that it will be lots of fun, and that it will incorporate what they have studied for the last six weeks, giving them an opportunity to share the freedom of Christ with their friends. Explain that going to Elysia is like becoming a Christian. We are free from life as a slave to sin (like the people in Albadonia who are slaves to Niko). Since we are free, it is our job to go back into the world and tell others of the freedom they can have by turning to God for help. By bringing their friends to this game, they should be able to share about the freedom they have in Jesus Christ through natural conversation relating to the game.

Focus
This is a special event—an outreach game that allows students to share Christ's freedom with their friends.

57

THE PLANNING

Several things must happen in order for this to be a success:

1. Word must get out. Your students must know about and understand the event well in advance. Also, they must ask their friends to come. You might print up business cards with the event information on them so students can hand them to friends as invitations.

2. You will need the use of the entire church building, or at least enough of it to make the game interesting with a large area to search and several places to hide. This means securing permission from the leadership of your church (better to ask permission than forgiveness). If you explain the purpose of the game, it shouldn't be a problem.

3. Adult help. This is a MUST! Nothing will send this game into chaos faster than not having enough adults to keep the kids on task. This means finding adults, singles and college students to volunteer. These people will make up the Royal Guard, the Jailers and the Elysians. They will be instrumental in keeping the game focused and the property intact.

4. Everyone must understand the purpose. You need to make sure your students are on your page as far as the game's emphasis and that the adults understand what their role is in the game. Without clear vision, the game will turn into a glorified hide-and-seek.

THE SET-UP

There are four areas needed for the game:

1. Albadonia - The city itself is the hallways and (open) rooms of the church building. The students wander the halls and check rooms in hopes of finding Elysia.

2. Elysia - This is the students' goal. This room needs to be secluded and hard to find. You might make it someplace outside the building so students have to actually be led there by someone and cannot simply stumble upon it. Elysia is a party place, complete with music (that cannot be heard outside the room), food, drinks, and whatever else makes a great party. (Make sure there is always an adult in there to supervise the festivities.)

3. Jail - This is a barren room with only one door. Students in jail are separated from one another and cannot talk. There should be enough Guards inside to enforce the rules and not too many students that they overwhelm the Guards.

4. Torture Room - This small room should be near the jail. Anyone who has been to Elysia and is later caught is brought here. They should be

58   Bonus Session

"interrogated" about the location of Elysia. If they squeal, they are allowed to live in jail. If they refuse to divulge the information, inform them they have been executed and allow them to return to Elysia, but they cannot leave there again.

BE SURE to secure the building before the game. This means locking any rooms that are off limits to students and putting away any valuable church property. Hopefully, no one will steal anything, but there is no sense in running the risk. Also, it is smart to put away any phones that could be used for calls to China or the Spice Girls Chat Line. Recheck the rooms a few times during the game to make sure they remain locked.

THE RULES

When everyone arrives, hand out a strip of cloth, bracelet, necklace, anything they can wear that shows they are a slave of Niko. Take plenty of time to explain the game's rules, as much as necessary, to ensure that the game is orderly and has purpose and isn't just a bunch of kids running around in the dark.

The game is fairly simple. The students must search for Elysia. They can do this two ways: find it on their own, or have someone lead them to it. This would be easy except for the Royal Guards wandering the city streets (halls of the church). The Guards have complete power and can do anything to anyone they see. Anyone who disobeys their orders or who tries to escape is thrown in prison.

The best way to discover Elysia is to ask people where it is (but don't let the Guards hear you!). What makes this more difficult is the fact that one of their fellow commoners is a spy. (You must choose this person beforehand and make sure he [or she] knows not to throw everyone he meets in jail, but to be selective and devious.) On the other hand, students may get lucky and meet the one Royal Guard who is an Elysian in disguise. (This Guard will also allow a jailbreak or two so no one sits in jail for the entire game.)

Once students find Elysia, they take off their necklaces (or whatever) that denote their slavery to Niko. They can hang out or choose to go back into Albadonia and lead others to Elysia. They can leave to help others at any time. They cannot put their necklaces back on, though. If they are caught by the Royal Guard in Albadonia, they will be interrogated and given a death sentence.

Finally, take a few moments to ask the students to respect the building. This should be a fun night, and if they treat the building well, they will get to use the building for such activities in the future.

Begin the game by having the Royal Guards (who should be wearing something special—matching hats, red bandannas or togas—that indicate they are Guards) burst into the room and break up the meeting. "Public gatherings are illegal! Into the streets immediately or face arrest!"

THE PARTY

Once the game has gone on for 45 minutes to an hour (keep a pulse on the students' interest in the game to decide when to end it), take everyone to Elysia for a party. The party should be just that—fun with loud music and food. This should be very relaxed and will hopefully demonstrate that church is a fun place to be.

THE WRAP-UP

Since the point of this game is outreach, there are a few ways you can go about wrapping it up. Choose whichever option you feel most comfortable with or create your own.

DEBRIEFING

If you feel that some debriefing questions are appropriate, try the ones listed below at the party:

- **How did it feel to live in fear?**
- **For those of you who found Elysia, why did those who left decide to leave?**
- **Why did the rest of you stay?**
- **How did it feel to be tricked by (<u>undercover spy</u>)?**
- **Why did some of you trust (<u>undercover Elysian</u>)?**
- **What are some freedoms we enjoy in the United States that other countries don't have?**
- **Did this game make you appreciate your freedom a little more?**

SUNDAY SERVICE

Invite everyone to your next youth service. The focus of that service will be studying Galatians and drawing the analogies between the game and our freedom in Christ. Make sure to have a time of response to Christ's gift of salvation.

PERSONAL

Tell your students that the game doesn't end that night. They need to hang out with their friends the next week and talk with them about the game and what it really means. Though this is the least likely choice to get the gospel message to everyone, it will probably have the highest impact on those who do hear it. It will also get your students to live the faith they have learned so much about in the last six weeks.

Whichever method you choose, make it a fun event for everyone. They will see that church can be fun and will be open to coming to other events. Also, this might turn into an annual outreach event. God's best to you as you enjoy your freedom!

OthEr EmpOweReD YouTh PrOduCts fRom StAndaRd PubLisHing

SOME KIND OF JOURNEY
VIDEO CURRICULUM

This innovative video curriculum is divided into seven segments perfect for youth group discussion. Included with the 90-minute video is a leader's guide to help you challenge your teens to grapple with the same issues that are discussed on the video—things like absolutes, swearing, homosexuality. Also included is a coupon good for $2.00 off any number of copies of the companion book, SOME KIND OF JOURNEY: ON THE ROAD WITH AUDIO ADRENALINE.

order # 03318
(UPC 7-07529-03318-1)

SOME KIND OF JOURNEY
ON THE ROAD WITH AUDIO ADRENALINE

By Jim Burgen, Ginny McCabe and Dale Reeves

Seven strangers from across the country spent a week on the road with one of today's hottest Christian bands, Audio Adrenaline. Why? To talk about seven relevant issues that concern today's youth—such as depression, sex, prejudice and divorce. Includes an AudioVision CD with interactive discussions, songs, videos and more! You'll also get behind-the-scenes tour photos of the band and the seven people who journeyed with them.

order # 03304
(ISBN 0-7847-0744-8)

WHAT I WISH MY YOUTH LEADER KNEW ABOUT YOUTH MINISTRY
A NATIONAL SURVEY

By Mike Nappa
Foreword by Rebecca St. James

A must-have resource for any junior- and senior-high youth worker! Mike Nappa, a 16-year youth ministry veteran, asked over 400 teens from across the nation about specific areas of youth ministry, such as worship, small groups, games, retreats and mission projects. His survey includes opinions from both of America's two youngest groups: GenX and the Millennial Generation. This 208-page book reveals the results of some of the most common questions about youth ministry asked by youth leaders: "How much of my ministry is run in a hit-or-miss fashion?", "Are my methods working?" and "How do I know that teenagers really want or need the programs I am investing so much time in?"

Order # 23331
(ISBN 0-7847-0911-4)

ALIEN INVASION
A CREATIVE STUDY OF THE BOOK OF EPHESIANS

By Michael Warden

This six-session elective for junior- and senior-high teens will help your students understand their new identity in Christ and launch a fresh invasion in their own lives. Each session features reproducible student sheets, contemporary Christian music suggestions, a midweek guide for personal devotions and numerous options! Also includes a bonus event that will let students spread God's Word to others in a strategic way.

Order # 23312
(ISBN 0-7847-0762-6)

BRAVE HEARTS
A CREATIVE STUDY OF THE BOOK OF JOSHUA

By Jane Vogel

This six-session elective course is designed to help senior-high teens discover that God can help them defeat the giants they face and tear down the walls in their lives. Creative teaching methods and activities will challenge students to boldly serve God. Each session features reproducible student sheets, contemporary Christian music suggestions, a midweek guide for personal devotions and ideas for student-led teaching! Also includes a bonus "commissioning" service.

Order # 23314
(ISBN 0-7847-0904-1)

TO ORDER, CONTACT YOUR LOCAL CHRISTIAN BOOKSTORE.

(IF THE BOOK IS OUT OF STOCK, YOU CAN ORDER BY CALLING 1-800-543-1353.)